Your Other Right

To Stephanie and Jorge,
Thank You Both For Your Kindness,
caring and compassion!
Your love and Zest For Life
is wonderful!
It is an Honor To Know
You Both!

Be well
Be Peaceful
Be Happy
Namasté

Mike Zerner

Genna

Your Other Right

Thoughts on Living a
Successful and Happy Life

Yoga, Yoems and *More*

Michael Zerner

Epigraph Books
Rhinebeck, New York

Images from freepik.com and Shutterstock.

ISBN 978-1-951937-95-9

Library of Congress Control Number 2021900812

Epigraph Books
22 East Market Street, Suite 304
Rhinebeck, NY 12572
(845) 876-4861
epigraphps.com

Contents

"TRUE YOGA IS NOT ABOUT THE SHAPE OF YOUR BODY,
BUT THE SHAPE OF YOUR LIFE.

YOGA IS NOT TO BE PERFORMED;
YOGA IS TO BE LIVED.

YOGA DOESN'T CARE ABOUT WHAT YOU HAVE BEEN;
YOGA CARES ABOUT THE PERSON YOU ARE BECOMING.

YOGA IS DESIGNED FOR A VAST AND PROFOUND PURPOSE,
AND FOR IT TO BE TRULY CALLED YOGA, ITS ESSENCE MUST BE EMBODIED."

Aadil Palkhivala

designed by freepik

Introduction

Thank you for opening this book; it was written for you.

This book is about exploring and learning new skills that will be with you for the rest of your life.

Success leaves clues; clues such as consistently dedicating your life to exercising your mind, body and spirit.

Yoga is one of the oldest forms of practice to exercise your mind, body and spirit.

Yoga will change your life.

Yoga will help you gain confidence, to respect yourself and all others...

Yoga will help you to appreciate all of life; everything and everyone, everywhere.

We are all on this Magnificent Planet Together!

So have fun learning, playing and exploring how to stay healthy and happy every day for the rest of your life!

This begins your world of Yoga, a world that will show you the path to won-drous delights!

Chapter One

You and I Are the Same

You and I are the same, no matter what we look like, no matter our shape, color or size.

We all have wonderful similarities, and beautiful differences!

We all have a story to tell.

We all want our voices to be heard.

Our lives are continuously full of ups and downs, it's important to have tools to use, to uplift us.

To help guide and teach us how to live our lives successfully and peacefully, with love, compassion and respect.

There are so many teachers and leaders that have, and will continue to guide us, shape us, and inspire us.

People's stories of perseverance, stamina, failures, and success, gives each of us road maps, the wisdom and strength to move forward.

To make lemonade from lemons!

The story I want to share with you is a story like yours, with ups and downs, with sorrows and triumphs, with battles, trials and tribulations, failures and successes.

It is in these lessons that we learn from gain and loss, from pleasure and sorrow, from fear and pain. It is these lessons that paves our way to happiness.

Believe In Yourself!

You've Got This!

You Can Do This!

We Believe in You!

Chapter Two

Welcome to "Your Other Right"

In yoga class while teaching, I see so many students going to their left when we say go to your right, many of us simply forget our left from our right. So, I often jokingly say, "Go the opposite way, your other right".

Hence the title!

Hopefully, this book will make you smile, laugh, grow and learn.

The purpose of this book is to give you the opportunity to go to any page and gain some thoughts on living life to your fullest!

It will offer tips to do your best, while feeling happy and strong.

Your life is a true test of your incredible ability to survive, to thrive!

To be your best!

You have many special abilities, your own unique gifts that you bring to this world.

We honor and appreciate you!

Thank you for sharing your distinctive qualities with everyone.

Thank you for wanting to help yourself to become better.

Thank you for wanting to make This World A Better Place!

Hopefully, this book will help you get to where you want to be,

Physically, Mentally and Spiritually.

Be Well.

Be Peaceful.

Be Happy.

Chapter Three

What is a Yoem?

"What is a yoem you ask"?

"I have never heard of a yoem you say.

"Never heard of such a thing, not today, not tomorrow, not yesterday."

Well of course that is true, because it is something I have created just for you.

A yoem is about the lessons of yoga written in rhyme.

Yoems help teach us yoga poses and philosophies in simple ways.

Yoems help us understand yoga inside and out.

Yoems help us figure things out.

Yoems provide us with insight, with knowledge of life.

Yoems help us navigate through life's' turmoil's and strife.

Explore yoga through these yoems and have fun.

Do it once in a while, or maybe every day, any which way.

Have fun reading these yoems, understanding the principles and knowledge yoga provides.

These yoems will prepare you to become a better person in every way, every day.

Chapter Four

Life is a Beautiful Ride

Have you ever had someone look at you, and ask, "What is wrong with you?"

"Why do you look or sound like that?"

Or maybe they ask, "Why are you different?"

If you have, you can understand the pain and discomfort of being different.

But guess what,

We Are All Different!

Everyone.

But life's lessons teach us to be strong, to persevere.

You will learn to embrace and value your uniqueness, your differences!

It may take time, but keep working at it

Believe in yourself!

You Can be Anybody you want!

You Can Achieve Anything your mind sets out to do!

You've got this!

You can do this!

Remember: Success leaves clues.

It is through our individual struggles that we must look to lessons shared.

Stories of success and wisdom have been passed on to us over the years through our teachers, our family, our friends, our acquaintances, people we know and people we don't; from history itself.

These lessons are here to help us create our greatest life!

Inside this book, you will find yoga poems, (yoems) yoga poses, positive thoughts and health tips that will take you, your mind, body and spirit to new heights, to new explorations, to new horizons!!

It will take you on a journey to a wonderful life!

What fun it is to share this wonderful ride with you!

You will come to see how disciplines like yoga, meditation, exercise, reading, writing and pursuing what you love is so beneficial to your daily happiness.

You will learn how helping others will be so rewarding, you will want to continue to keep helping others in any way you can.

So have fun and be creative in your pursuit of achieving fantastic health and wellness, have fun and enjoy an improved physical and emotional state of well-being in every way.

Every Day!

Yoga is so much fun to do, while being incredibly beneficial too!

Try it.

You'll like it! I Promise.

Yoga is a discipline that teaches balance, breath, strength, love, respect, health, charity, humility, discipline, exploration, community and exercise of your mind, body and spirit, all in one!!

There are many favorable characteristics and traits obtained through yoga; you will find that it puts you on a path to continually giving your all, your very best!

Yoga teaches us:

To Never Quit. To Never Give Up!

Improving yourself daily is the key to success and achievement.

Immerse yourself in the lifelong pursuit of wanting to live every moment of every day, in every way.

Enjoy your pursuit of creating for yourself, positive energy, seeking to continuously explore, working to continuously improve yourself every moment.

Believe In Yourself!

You've Got This!

You Can Do This!

Have Fun!

Enjoy The Ride!

designed by freepik.com

Chapter Five

This is My Story; This is Your Story

This is my story, hopefully it will inspire you, your family and friends. I have had an unusually long list of health issues my entire life.

At a young age I encountered and battled allergies, asthma, and respiratory problems. As I got into my teens and early twenties, and to this day, I have had countless operations, hundreds of procedures and many, many setbacks.

Seemingly going back two steps to move forward by only one.

But everyone has their own problems.

All of us have choices to either quit and give up, or keep moving forward, no matter how slow or how fast your progress will be.

My back, shoulders, and knees, in addition to other parts, have had multiple operations. I have battled two forms of cancer. Undergoing these countless procedures has been a challenge to say the least.

Throw in a crooked face, crooked smile, a crooked spine, constant redness in my right eye, and you can see why young kids continually ask me "What's up with you, Why do you look like that?"

Ah, the honesty of children!

Kids tell it like it is!

As it should be!

My back has collapsed by over five and half inches, leading to overcoming many obstacles in simply moving.

Like all of us facing challenges, this often leads to many insecurities, fear, failure and anxiety.

But remember,....

We Can and Must Turn Lemons Into Lemonade!

We need only embrace our differences, relish in them and see them as positives, not negatives.

Via La Difference!

A Traves De La Diferencia!

> "SELF-PITY IS OUR WORST ENEMY AND IF WE YIELD TO IT,
> WE CAN NEVER DO ANYTHING GOOD IN THE WORLD."
>
> Helen Keller

We do have choices though, we can wallow in self pity,

Or,

We can accept it and move on, knowing...

That No One Is Perfect.

Therefore, we all must keep trying, keep working to overcome, to not give in.

Everyone is battling something.

We all must keep going, continue on, live one moment at a time and your life will be a wonderful, magical, celebration of life!

A life filled with peace, love, compassion, honesty, and harmony within.

Your confidence and self belief will radiate a force field of light and love that will surround you. This light, will be palpable to others. People will see your great health and happiness, they will see and feel your smile, your warmth, your sparkle, your glow.

They will sense your great respect for everything and everyone, they will feel your kindness for them, and for all of life!

Appreciate your differences, accept and enjoy your challenges.

Throughout your life, you will continually grow.

You will become abundant in every way.

Through your learnings and through your hard work, you will give back to so many who need you as their teacher, who appreciate what you have achieved.

Through your kindness and caring, you will become a mentor, role model and teacher to many.

You are passing it forward!

We are proud of you and your hard work, we are proud to share our story with you.

Thank you for picking up this book.

And Remember....

Always believe in yourself!

Always Belief That You Are Getting Better In Every Way, Every Day!

Chapter Six

Yoga Teaches Us to Be Here Now

Yoga teaches us to live in the moment, one breath at a time.

Challenges will always come your way, that is simply life.

But yoga will help you in overcoming these obstacles.

It will help you explore, understand and conquer whatever physical and mental setbacks you have.

These challenges will test you.

But, don't give up, don't quit.

Study, investigate, educate yourself.

The answers to what troubles you will always be available to you, they will always be found inside yourself. Listen to your heart, your intuition, your soul.

Be still and listen to your true self.

Be still and know.

Chapter Seven

Let the Yoems Begin

YOUR OTHER RIGHT

Your Other Right:
Sometimes we know right from left,
Sometimes right from wrong,
Sometimes we feel weak.
Sometimes we feel strong.
Sometimes we make mistakes.
Sometimes we do well.
Sometimes we fall and stumble
But always remain humble.
Keep getting up when you fall,
Fall down seven times, get up eight!
Stand proud and tall.
Keep getting up,
And all will be well.

designed by freepik.com

Chapter Eight

Together

Men are called Yogis, Woman are called Yoginis,
Together we are all yogi's.
We are all created equal.
We are all one.
Having both feminine and masculine traits within each of us,
We share characteristics that represent our collective qualities.
Incorporating our different strengths from each,
We bond together.
With respect, love and unity.
Equal and free, our world is one.
Dreaming of possibilities.
We are blessed, with diversity, with differences, and with similarities.
It is in us all, everyone, everywhere.
Together we form life.
Together we form humanity.
Together we must take care of our Planet
Our World.
Now, not later.
Today before it's too late.
Don't wait or hesitate to lend your environmental support.
We are destroying our home,
Our People
Our Animals
Our Flora
Our Fauna.

We must all work together
So we may leave our Precious World To Future Generations.
Leaving a planet that is renewable and sustainable in very way.
A healthy Planet. Growing, Thriving,
Healthy in Every Way.

"THE EARTH DOES NOT BELONG TO MAN; MAN BELONGS TO THE EARTH. THIS WE KNOW. ALL THINGS ARE CONNECTED LIKE THE BLOOD WHICH UNITES ONE FAMILY. WHATEVER BEFALLS THE EARTH BEFALLS THE SONS AND DAUGHTERS OF THE EARTH. MAN DID NOT WEAVE THE WEB OF LIFE, HE IS MERELY A STRAND IN IT. WHATEVER HE DOES TO THE WEB, HE DOES TO HIMSELF."

Chief Seatlle

Chapter Nine

Yoga Poses/Asanas

Surya Namaskar

'Surya' = 'Sun'   'Namaskar' ='Respect'

Sun Salutation

Twelve postures there are.

Each asana allows your mind and spirit to travel far.

Exploring each pose, rising and folding, up and down you go.

Exploring each pose separately, then collectively, having fun with the sun.

Let go.

Salute the sun, and you will see,

The sun always gives back, now its' her time to receive.

Give back to the sun.

Having fun, you'll appreciate your surroundings.

The Glorious sky, the marvelous earth, the majesty of the sea.

Salute the sun when your day has begun.

Benefits

+   Weight Loss
+   Glowing skin
+   Cardio
+   Improves blood circulation

Tips

+   Practice Sun Salutation A first, then B, then C
+   Do this sequence at least four times
+   Do this as a flow, a dance

Balasana

'Bala' = 'Child'   'Asana' = 'Pose'

Child pose

Curl into a ball,
Begin with your head and chin tucked in.
Your arms behind you to the side, feel the security and safety as if
you're in your mother's womb.
Safe and secure from head to toes.
Balasana, is the universal peaceful pose.
It creates a calmness with in,
A peaceful way.
So enjoy the security, comfort and serenity that this pose will bring
you today.

Benefits

+ Reduces stiffness and opens up
  the spine
+ Relaxes and calms the mind
+ Great for the hips

Tips

+ Inhale oxygen bubbles up your
  spine, exhale like an accordion
  out through your sides.
+ Separate your knees wide as
  feels comfortable.
+ Relax your forehead on your
  mat or block.

Marjaryasana/Bitilasana

'Marjari' = 'Cat'   'Bitila' ='Cow'

Cat/cow

I am cat, Marjaryasana said I.

I am cow, Bitilasana said I.

The cat says;

First I arch my back, sigh a meow, then I bow my head, looking between my paws,

it feels so good, my back arches round, making a soothing, purring sound, my smile profound.

Then I drop my belly down.

The cow says,

While looking up, moo I breathe, loud and long, now I am the cow.

I am strong.

How wonderful to move up and down, oiling up my hip hinges.

Flowing free and calm.

Benefits

+ Excellent for helping with your back, neck and torso.
+ Massages the internal organs

Tips

+ Keep the crease line of your wrists straight.
+ Exhale while pulling your belly in for the cat
+ Inhale from your shoulder blades down in the cow

Vrikasana

'Vrksa' = 'Tree'   'Asana' ='Pose'

Tree

I am a tree tall and strong, standing in Vrikasana
With my arms extended long, reaching for the sky while my foot
reaches firmly down, like tree roots, rooted firmly into the ground.
Bringing up my opposite foot to my inner thigh, balancing on one leg,
I am a tree, feeling tall and strong.
Sometimes I sway, it just depends on the day.
And that's OK.
Never waver, believe in yourself, have faith, go out on a limb.
Simply balance your life the best you can, in every way, every day.
Stand like a Tree, you'll be happy as you gently sway.

Benefits

+ Improves balance and stability
+ Strenthens feet, legs, hips
+ Builds self-confidence

Tips

+ Find a "Drishti", this is your focus. Focus on a unmoving point in front of you.
+ Press your foot against your leg, and your leg against your foot, for greater balance
+ Your standing leg is your tree trunk, your satnding foot are your roots to Mother Earth

Khanjanasana

'Khanjana' = 'Wag tail'   'Asana' ='Pose'

Wagging Dog Pose

I am a dog, I am your best friend.
On my hands and knees am I
Wagging my tail, makes me smile.
I bet you'd be happy too if you did the same for a while.
Without fail, you should try.
It will make you feel wonderful,
This is not a lie.
You'll even let out a relaxing bark and sigh, saying I'm so glad I tried.
Unconditional love are you, just like a happy dog.
In the end, you'll constantly be wagging your tail,
Smiling from head to toe, through and through.

Benefits

+ Opens up hips
+ Lubricates the lower spine
+ Allows you to be in the moment, happy like your dog.

Tips

+ Make sure spine is like a table top, with a straight spine.
+ Place cushions or pads under your knees if they hurt

Adho Muhka Svanasana

'Adho' = 'Downward'   'Mukha' = 'Face'   'Svana' = 'Dog'

Downward Facing Dog

Into downward dog do I go, Adho Muhka Svanasana feels so nice.
Stretching from up to down, from the moon to the sun,
from the east to the west,
Downward dog feels so great, it's the best!
Shaking my coat,
Makes me feel good and strong, tall and long.
A wonderful sensation does it bring.
How fantastic!
You're so happy, you want to shout your happiness out loud,
you'll want to sing!
You strive to reach, to be the most you can be.
You are alive and raring to go.
Viewing the views, seeing all you can see in downward dog,
You're as young as a pup.
Being downward up!

Benefits

+ Calms the brain, relieves headaches
+ Improves face complexion
+ Reverse blood flow helps your body

Tips

+ Have your wrist in line with your forearm, forearm in line with your shoulders
+ The wider your legs, the easier it is on your hamstrings.

Adho Muhka Svanasana—Downward Facing Dog

Urdhva Mukha Svanasana

'Urdhava' = 'Upward'   **'Mukha' = 'Face'**   **'Asana' = 'Pose'**

Upward Facing Dog Pose

Upward facing dog, Urdhva Mukha Svanasana am I.
Stretching my legs off the ground, arching my back way up;
Looking to the sky, my body stretching, my legs long.
My arms and legs are becoming so strong.
Some days I can hold this pose all day long.
I feel tall and happy, wonderfully smiling, knowing I belong.
I stretch to the sky, my head looking up far and wide.
Upward dog I become,
Letting go, matters not where, just going with the flow.
Here, there, everywhere.
Watch me run, glide and go.

Benefits

+ Elongates your spine.
+ Improves posture
+ Builds strong gluts

Tips

+ Do not strain your neck while looking up
+ Press on the palms of your hands, the fleshy part of your hands
+ Draw shoulders away from your ears

Sirasana

'Sirsa' = 'Head'   'Asana' = 'Pose'

Headstand

You lay on your head, comfortable as if you were in bed.

Upside down, without a frown.

King of all asanas is Sirasana, to stand on your head, a crowning achievement.

This is the way to be, releasing the blood flow down to your head so effortlessly.

Life's lessons leaves clues.

If you only knew that lying upside down took away the blues, you'd do it every day,

this is so true.

From upside down, enjoy this most wonderful view.

Benefits

+ Stimulates the pituitary and pineal glands
+ Tones the core
+ Improves digestion

Tips

+ Interlace your fingers, place the crown of your head in your hands
+ Use a wall for support to begin with
+ Place 90 percent of your weight on your arms shoulders, your neck is relaxed

Sirasana—Headstand

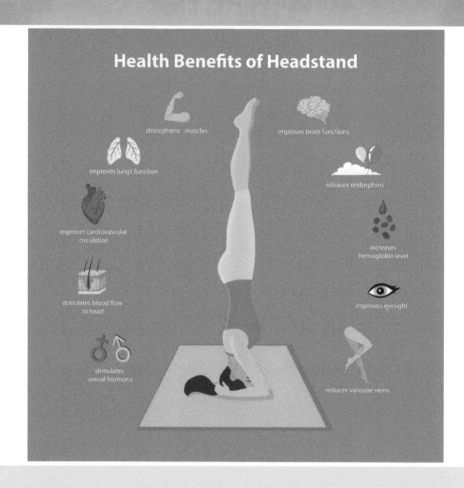

Tadasana

'Tada' = 'Mountain'   'Asana' = 'Pose'

Mountain

Standing in Tadasana you are bold.
Mountain pose is like savasana standing up, not
lying down.
A foundation pose, this asana leads to so many
others, mountain will bring you strength,
Length, beauty, poise and peace.
Feeling the balance in your feet, the base of your
mountain becomes firm.
Your spine is straight, your demeanor calm.
Reaching to the summit, the very top, you feel
the aura above.
You know no limits.
You handle all that life has to give.
You are emboldened, wise, serene, you know
right from wrong.
You are a mountain, with all her majesty, you are
tall and strong!

Benefits

+ Strengthens legs
+ Improves posture
+ Helps with flat feet

Tips

+ Stand tall and straight
+ Military attention
+ Head over heart, heart over hips

Eka Pada Rajakopatasana

'Eka' = 'One'   'Pada' = 'Foot'   'Raja' = "King'   'Kapota' = "Pigeon'

King of the Pigeon

Pigeons show us a pose we all know so well.

Eka Pada Rajakopapotasana is it's Sanskrit name.

One-legged King of the Pigeon it is also called, is the same.

It seems difficult, but truly it is tame.

Your one leg slides forward on your mat, that front foot forming a right angle on the ground, you slide you're other leg straight back descending your thigh to the floor.

Keep your hands on your hips as you begin.

Sit up tall with a big grin.

Feel your hips relax, your pelvic bowl open.

A sense of balance, it elicits many an emotion.

Enjoy the stretch, enjoy the fun.

Experiencing the pigeon pose will bring you positivity, you'll want to keep going.

Relishing the energy of this pose and all that yoga provides,

Embracing yoga for the rest of your life,

Will lead you to enjoy many magical rides.

Benefits

+   Strengthens thighs, quads, and psoas muscles
+   Opens up chest
+   Opens up shoulders

Tips

+   Keep hips in alignment
+   Use a blanket under a hip if you need it
+   Use a belt for your back foot if needed

Eka Pada Rajakopatasana——King of the Pigeon

Bhekasana

'Bheka' = 'Frog'   **'Asana' = 'Pose'**

Frog

Ribbit say I.
Who might I be?
Bhekasana the frog of course, can't you see?
I lye on my frog belly with my frog legs wide apart,
My toes and feet reach towards my ears,
Making me forever young in years.
Man do I feel my inner thighs!
The adductors are saying " my oh my."
Just relax, breath and sigh.
Opening up your hips in frog, makes them more flexible, more free,
strong and alive!
So let the magic happen,
A clearing will be revealed.
Lying in frog today,
Your happiness is sealed.

Benefits

+ Helps with inner thighs
+ Lowers stress
+ Lowers anxiety

Tips

+ Turn toes up towards your ears
+ You can place a blanket or block
  under your chest

Ardha-Bhekasana

'Ardha' = 'Half'   'Bheka' = 'Frog'

Half-Frog

Stretch your hips for strength and flexibility.
Add Ardha-Bhekasana, half frog to your yoga routine.
Getting on your knees, bend and lift one leg at a time.
Just like male dogs do. Don't be shy.
Whether a gal or a guy,
All in one pose it is,
A frog on one knee, you are a fire hydrant too.
Practice the frog often; it's so good for you.

Benefits

+ Tones your hips
+ Tones your inner thighs
+ Tones your core

Tips

+ Keep your lifted leg, foot and ankle parallel with each other.
+ Keep your arms strong and engaged

Salamba Sarvangasana

'Salamba' = 'With support'   'Sarvanga' = 'All'

Shoulder Stand

Shoulder Stand is fun,
I find myself looking up to the sky, the stars, the moon, the sun.
The Queen of all poses, it's great to do, it's fantastic for your body too!
You'll love it, yes you will.
Salamba Sarvangasana is the
Sanskrit name,
Looking upside down is your
view, your aim.
Seldom do we reverse our blood
flow, lying upside down in
Shoulder Stand your body will
feel that wonderful glow!
With your hands on the small of
your back
Straighten your legs to the sky
From here, there are so many
things to do.
You can spread your legs wide
taking each leg back to its oppo-
site side,

Benefits

+ Reverse blood flow
+ Improves complexion
+ Tones buttocks and legs

Tips

+ Make sure your neck is relaxed
+ Place a folded blanket under
  your shoulders to help your
  neck
+ Squeeze an imaginary towel
  between your anles, knees and
  thighs

Salamba Sarvangasana—Shoulder Stand

Then bend your legs with your feet together like a butterfly,
Turn your toes down to your nose.
Then glide your legs back up again,
Have fun in Shoulder Stand, enjoy your ride,
From all around, down to up,
Your feet reaching the sky!
Look Ma no hands!

Ardah Pincha Mayurasana

'Ardha' = 'Half'   'Pincha' = 'Feathered'

Dolphin

Dolphins swim long and far.
Smart they are.
They are always grinning, smiling too.
Life is but a game to them.
Come, let's play they say.
Play with us today!
So, get on your forearms and raise your dolphin tail to the sky.
Lower your heels down to the ground.
Hold tight your girth, your core is strong
Pretend you are a dolphin in the water,
Having fun all day long!

Benefits

+ Calms mind
+ Reduces depression
+ Total body strength building

Tips

+ Stay strong in your forearms
+ Stay strong in your legs

Makara Adho Mukha Svanasana

'Makara' = "Crocodile"　　　'Mukha' ='Facing'　　　'Asana' ='Pose'

'Adhas' = 'Down'　　　'Svana' ='Dog'

Dolphin Plank

From Dolphin come into a plank,

As you get strong you will have yourself to thank!

Rest on your forearms and elbows, stay for a while

Hold your abs, your bum tight and firm,

Feeling strong! Feel the burn!

Soon you'll be sporting a strong core, a six pack and more!

Your confidence will grow,

Your overall health will improve, your spirit will soar!

You will enjoy each day more and more.

Benefits

+ Improves core strength
+ Improves your gluts
+ Stamina

Tips

+ Maintain your alignment like a plank of wood
+ Focus on a spot on your mat or the floor

Simhasana

'Simha' = 'Lion'   'Asana' = 'Pose'

Lion

Roar says the mighty cat, Roar!!
This is the call of the Lion. Simhasana is the pose.
Creating your own voice, letting your own voice be heard.
Strong are you, fierce and proud, different, not weird.
Roar Out loud! I say Roar!
It's wonderful for you to scream it out,
Letting out your emotions
through your voice,
As long as you're yourself,
you will always be confi-
dent, perfect and more.
So, let's all scream and
ROARRRRRRR!

Benefits

+ Relieves tension in face and chest
+ Helps with sore throats by stimulating the platysma
+ Curbs stress

Tips

+ As you exhale open up your eyes and stick out your tongue
+ Engage your fists and then release them onto the ground

Navasana

'Nava' = 'Boat'   'Asana' = 'Pose'

Full Boat

Navasana- you are now in the full boat pose.

At first your tummy will be sore.

It's so good for your body, so good for strength.

It will tighten your belly up. No more jelly around your core.

Keep practicing and you'll want to do more and more and more!

This pose will become part of your yoga routine.

Your back will improve. Your posture will as well.

You will feel like a million bucks, maybe a million and two!

Practice Navasana, the boat pose, and your body will feel brand new!

Benefits

+ Engages your core
+ Reduces back stress
+ Helps to focus on a challenge and calm nerves

Tips

+ Keep your stomach and back muscles engaged
+ Focus on a spot
+ With arms extended out, spread your fingers for energy

Salabasana

'Salaba' = 'Locust'   'Asana' = 'Pose'

Locust

Super Man, Super Woman is this pose. Salabhasana is the Sanskrit name.

This feels so good, after doing this once or twice, you'll never feel the same.

Becoming mighty and bold, this asana never gets old.

Starting on your belly, supine, rise up with your forehead, chin and chest, raise your legs too, fly your arms back and feel free!

Doing this will keep you young in heart and strong in your spine, flying with your arms and legs off the ground always feels fantastic!

So fly and climb and soar!

Benefits

+ Improves posture
+ Stretches shoulders, chest and belly
+ Stimulates organs

Tips

+ Focus on a spot
+ Raise your arms parallel to the floor, stretch back through your fingertips
+ Press your scapula

Dhanurasana

'Dhanu' = 'Bow'   'Asana' = 'Pose'

Bow

A bow is what you are.
Holding on to your feet with each hand, you lift and glide into the
bow.
Rocking back and forth you go.
Dhanurasana, the Wheel it is called
To give your life the energy it needs,
Do the bow and you will feel wonderful, tremendous and more!
You'll feel marvelous,
Knowing that all is well!

Benefits

+ Helps with weight loss
+ Improves digestion
+ Improves blood circulation

Tips

+ Reach back for one foot at a time.
+ Gently rock back and forth
+ Take out focus on a spot and with your arms extended out, spread your fingers for energy

Akarma Dhanurasana

'Karna' = 'Ear'   'Dhanur' = 'Bow'   'Asana' = 'Pose'

Archer

Akarma Dhanurasana, the archer will build strength, forging a keen eye.

Doing this pose will bring you great self-esteem,

Allowing everything to be in its place, to be as it should, as it seems.

Like the Archer, take hold of your toe with your peace fingers,

Remember don't let go.

Bring your foot to your ear like an archer brings the arrow and string back,

Hold for a while, feeling your comfort, but also your strength,

Grinning ear to ear,

Your smile is as wide and as long as a mile!

Benefits

+ Opens up the heart chakra
+ Balances the nervous system
+ Energizes the body

Tips

+ If unable to reach your extended foot, use a belt
+ Sit up tall and straight
+ Pull back top bent leg toward your ear

Virabhadrasana I

'Vira' = 'Hero'   'Bhadra' = 'Friend'   'Asana' = 'Pose'

Warrior I

Standing tall and proud you are a mighty Warrior,
With this there is no doubt.
Reaching your arms to the sky while bending your forward knee,
You become fierce and confident, mighty and strong,
You are a warrior battling all wrongs.
Practicing this pose, you will forever be,
That mighty Warrior that every person sees.

Benefits

+ Strengthens entire body
+ Boosts stamina
+ Relieves back aches

Tips

+ Your front heel is in alignment with your back arch. Your back foot is your anchor
+ Focus on a spot
+ With arms extended out, spread your fingers for energy

Virabhadrasana II

'Vira' = 'Hero'   'Bhadra' = 'Friend'   'Asana' = 'Pose'

Warrior II

Proud Warrior calls you forth to believe.
To believe in yourself.
To be proud, to be free.
To believe in yourself,
And not what others think.
No one is beneath you; no one is better than you.
You are beneath no one, we are all equals,
This is true, that over time you learn,
That valuable lessons are not to be spurned.
Fearless in the face of all challenges,
Standing in the Warrior I pose, turn
your waist to the side,
Parallel with your mat.
With your arms outstretched,
bend your front knee,
Looking over your forward arm,
Extending, reaching forward,
Looking over your fingers,
Find your focus.
Now notice the pride in your stride.

Benefits

+ Engages hips
+ Engages arms
+ Increase focus

Tips

+ Keep hips parallel to the side of your mat
+ Don't lean to your right, nor left, feel the pose equally in both hips
+ Squeeze your shoulder blades together

Virabhadrasana III

'Vira' = 'Hero'   'Bhadra' = 'Friend'   'Asana' = 'Pose'

Warrior III

Like I and II, this asana will let you soar and fly.
Standing in Warrior I simply lift one leg and take it straight back behind you,
Parallel off the floor, with your arms reaching forward,
Balancing on one leg you'll fly.
Loving this feeling of strength and happiness,
You are building confidence and delight.
You're a bird in flight!
You won't be questioning yourself,
You'll be living your life,
Your way.
Never having to ask permission,
Not doubting yourself,
Trust and believe in your convictions,
Trust and believe in yourself.
Warrior III will let you fly today,
It will take you a very long way!

Benefits

+ Helps increase balance
+ Strengthens balancing leg
+ Improves concentration

Tips

+ Keep your stomach and back muscles engaged
+ Focus on a spot
+ With arms extended out, spread your fingers for energy

Virabhadrasana III—Warrior III

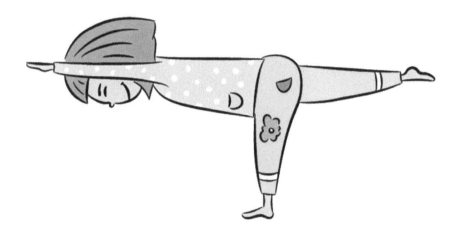

Malasana

'Mala' = 'Garland'   'Asana' = 'Pose'

Bug

Bug.Bug. Bug.
A bug loves to bug bug bug around.
Squatting down into Malasana, with your arms inside and through your legs,
Take hold of your ankles, then you gently move side to side.
Enjoy the stretch; it's a free ride.
It will give you balance and strength in your legs.
Your hips become strong as well.
When you are done with the pose,
Stand slowly back up into rag doll,
uttanasana.
This will help you counter the pose, to regain your length.
To become long and tall.
In the bug, bug bug you will have a ball!

Benefits

+   Stretches torso
+   Increases leg strength
+   Increase flexibility

Tips

+   Squat down slowly
+   Keep your hips engaged
+   Use a block for your hands if it is hard coming to namaste' hands

Uttanasana

'Ut' = 'Intense'   'Tan'='To Extend'   'Asana' = 'Pose'

Rag Doll

You bend from the hips, not the waist
Folding over, relaxing, letting go.
Grab your elbows if you like and sway to and fro.
You'll feel so relaxed,
Smiling wide, up and down, never wearing a frown.
Hanging in Rag Doll simply let go; leave all your worries and woes on the ground,
Leave your problems on the floor, show them out the door.
Let them slip away into the universe,
Through your fingertips and toes,
Your worries are never more.
You don't need them today,
Any day,
Or anymore.

Benefits

+ Improves digestion
+ Increases oxygen intake
+ Relax tired muscles

Tips

+ Forward fold from your hips, not your waist
+ Pull down your elbows, relax your head
+ Release your arms like a rag doll

Kurmasana

'Kurm' = 'Tortoise'   'Asana' = 'Pose'

Turtle

Begin siting on your mat with your legs forming a diamond.
Threading your arms under your bent knees, feet together
Like two pages of an open book.
Spread your arms under your legs as wide as you can.
You'll find your torso folding forward.
Remember you are a turtle so take it slow.
Only forward fold to a comfortable level,
Only as far as you want to go.
Remember you are turtle, so take it nice and slow.

Benefits

+ Improves digestion and respiratory functions
+ Opens up hips
+ Helps with shoulders

Tips

+ Only forward fold to your comfort
+ You can round your back
+ Extend arms under your legs only as far as you want

Garundasana

'Garuda' = 'Eagle'   'Asana' = 'Pose'

Eagle

Fly like an Eagle,
Then fly some more.
With your arms flying up towards the sky, cross them over.
Your right arm goes under your left, then raise your elbows up.
Lift up your right leg and tuck your toes behind your left calf.
Do both sides.
Flying high you can see far and wide,
Near and far.
You're an eagle flying on the thermals of the wind.
You're an eagle flying, having fun,
You're an eagle with a Huge
Smile and a Big Grin!

Benefits

+ Improves balance
+ Improves leg strength.
+ Improves arm flexibility
+ Improves balance

Tips

+ Raise crossed arms to your chest
+ Squat down comfortably
+ Focus your gaze

Parighasana

'Pariha'= 'Iron Bar used to Lock A Gate'   'Asana' ='Pose'

Gate Pose

Parighasana it is called.
Your gate will remain flexible and strong
When you practice this pose
You will continue to grow tall and long.
Kneel on the floor and straighten your left leg out to the left side.
Take your left arm and roll it down your left leg, feel your left arm
reaching down long.
Now extend your right arm over
your right ear to the sky
Feeling this wonderfully deep
side bend,
Your IT band will whisper thank
you again and again.
Its benefits are immense.
This pose brings harmony and
fortitude,
This pose knows no end.
Gate pose is fantastic!
A favorite pose,
A favorite friend.

Benefits

+ Increases adductors
+ Stretches intercoastal muscles
+ Beneficial for lungs

Tips

+ Have your palm facing down
  with your extended arm over
  your ear
+ Reach through your fingertips
+ Raise ball of foot if unable to
  flatten it on the mat

Chandra Namaskaskar

'Chandra' = 'Moon'   'Namaskar' = 'Respect'

Moon Salutation

A salute to the Moon.
She orbits around Mother Earth faithfully.
As we salute her, we bow to her gracefully.
There are many variations to this sequence.
Various as the differences in which we inhabitants make up our world.
No matter which order of movements you choose,
Doing the Moon Salutation often, you can't lose.
Preparing your body for a flow.
You rock and roll.
Your spirit soars, and yet,
You feel rooted to your core.
Your mind becomes peaceful and still.
Exploring your soul from the inside out.
From within and without,
Oh, you are a beautiful sight!
So, here's to the Moon
Like you, always shining bright!

Benefits

- Total body flow
- Paying respect to the Moon
- Cardio

Tips

- Choose different sequences
- Repeat at least four times
- Visualize doing this as a dance

Chandra Namaskaskar —Moon Salutation

Ustrasana

'Ustra' = 'Camel'   'Asana' = 'Pose'

The Camel

The camel am I, ustrasana
Reaching my arms up and back,
Touching my heels with each hand
I arch my head up, looking behind,
I smile and grin.
This is such a wonderful back bend
Such an enjoyable time.
Thanks to the camel
My back is healthy, supple, feeling divine!

Benefits

- Improves blood circulation to eyes and to your brain
- Improves the flexibility of your spine
- Activates the spleen and liver

Tips

- Place thumbs on your lower back, arch your head back
- For greater poses, place your hands on your heels while on top of your toes, or place toenails into the mat and touch your feet
- Keep thighs from going forward
- Squeeze your shoulders

Natarajasana

'Nata' = 'Dancer'   'Raja'='King'   'Asana'='Pose'

The Dancer

The Dancer.
Taking hold of the inside foot of my back leg,
I raise it up, up to the sky
My opposite arm soaring forward
Balancing
Dancing
I am smiling
Loving this asana, loving this
pose,
Natarasana provides me length,
strength,
Beauty and poise,
It is pure delight.
It makes you feel so much better.
So, light.
You are poetry in motion.
You prance,
Thank you, Dancer,
Thank you for this dance.

Benefits

+ Assists in weight loss
+ Strengthens legs
+ Improves balance

Tips

+ Take hold of inner ankle if possible when lifting up back leg
+ Keep standing leg firm
+ Use a strap for your back leg
+ Use a wall to help assist you

Savasana

'Sava' = 'Corpse'   'Asana' = 'Pose'

Corpse Pose

Lying supine,
We end each yoga class by lying still.
Almost sleeping if you will.
Scanning and feeling each body part from head to toe,
Relaxing each muscle, each organ, each bone and sinew, one by one.
This is the ultimate in calmness, serenity and ease.
Savasana is known as the resting pose,
The equivalent of hours of sleep.
It helps to quiet you muscles and your mind.
It's search leads to the Divine.
Peace is the destination.
Tranquility the final achievement,
The final goal.
The most perfect place.
Arising from Savasana,
You'll feel refreshed, energized and awake.
You'll seize the day, make no mistake,
You are ready to tackle whatever
comes your way,
Right Now, Today!

Benefits

+ It eases mental and physical stress
+ It helps ease depression
+ The mind, body, spirit and soul receives complete rest, peace and happiness

Tips

+ Make sure your body is in alignment from head to toe
+ Use an eye pillow or essential oils if you'd like
+ Focus on your body from head to toe, then focus on your breath

Chapter Ten

Thoughts on Living a Successful and Healthy Life

Helpful, Happy and Healthy Thoughts

Success leaves clues, this we know.

In order to build a Happy, Healthy and Successful Life, we must pay attention to these clues, these life lessons.

It is extremely important that we do.

Our largest organ in our body, is our skin, it is called plasticity.

Life's lessons teach us that drinking lots of water and exercising our bodies will lead to greater plasticity, and greater plasticity will lead to a better life.

Neuroplasticity is the functioning of our brain. Continually learning, expanding our brains' capabilities, keeps our minds active, alert, alive, healthy and happy. Learning new games, new languages, new sports, new music, is vital to improving our brains, to improving our lives.

The following lessons and tips on life will help you to improve your mind, to improve your body, to improve your spirit and to improve the overall quality of your life.

IT WILL HELP YOU TO:
LIVE A HEALTHY LIFE!

IT WILL HELP YOU TO:
LIVE YOUR VERY BEST LIFE.

Healthy Tip Number One

Live in the Moment

Live in the moment.
Embrace all you see, feel, hear, smell, taste,
Explore all your senses totally and completely.
Learn all the lessons of life you can, the good and the bad,
Ones that bring you happiness, along with those that make you sad.
Ones from your past and ones from the present,
These lessons will help you prepare for your future.
We know that prior preparation prevents poor performance.
But you can only prepare for the future in the present, in the moment.
Preparing for your future, will help prepare you for your next task.
It will lead you to success upon success!
Soon you will see, how living in this the moment will set you free.
Yard by yard, life is hard, but....
Inch by inch life is a cinch.
Realize and know, for you to be happy,
Being in the moment is the only place to be.

"LIFE CAN ONLY BE FOUND IN THE PRESENT
MOMENT.
THE PAST IS GONE.
THE FUTURE IS NOT YET HERE.
AND IF WE DO NOT GO BACK TO OURSELVES IN THE
PRESENT MOMENT,
WE CANNOT BE IN TOUCH WITH LIFE."

Thich Nhat Hanh

Healthy Tip Number Two

Drink plenty of water

Do you know that when you go to bed at night, your body is like a water tank, it is completely full.

Water provides your body and brain with energy, a source that allows us to become fresh and renewed.

Nourish yourself throughout your day.

Because when you awake, your body's water tank is low, low low.

Near empty, it's time to re-hydrate, refuel,

Time to get your body and brain back to be able to, Go, Go, Go!

Drinking water will improve you, in every way.

It will keep you well,

You'll be able to tell that you feel swell!

Drink a tall glass of refreshing water or two soon after you rise,

And continue to drink water, it will keep you energized, refreshed,

Renewed all day.

Your body, mind and spirit will thank you.

So off you go, on your way.

To explore, discover and enjoy.

Staying hydrated every day,

Your journey, your path in life will lead you to a better way.

Your life begins with your health,

So, stay the course,

And soon you'll be on your way to discover...

That Every Brand-New Day Is Delightful in Each And Every Way!

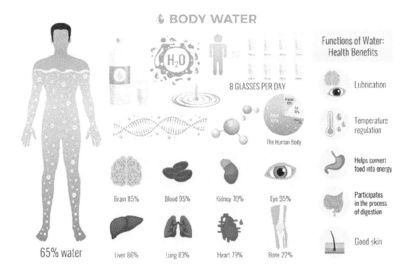

Healthy Tip Number Three

Keep moving.

Keep your body moving.

Respect your body, this incredible machine.

Maintain your skin, bones, joints, and your mind.

You are a complex, work of science, and so much more.

206 bones in our bodies, with up to 850 muscles too.

Keep your joints lubricated, they'll love you for this,

And they'll last a long time too!

Your body will be loose, mobile, and supple, you won't feel stiff like you're made of glue.

Keep moving, no matter what you do.

Keep moving, you'll enjoy it too.

Do it now.

Keep moving, each and every day anew.

It will help your mind, body and spirit soar to new heights,

Through and through,

Keep your body moving and see,

How much your life will feel balanced,

You will feel in the groove.

And oh, how your life will improve!

"IF YOU CAN'T FLY, THEN RUN,
IF YOU CAN'T RUN THEN WALK,
IF YOU CAN'T WALK THEN CRAWL,
BUT WHATEVER YOU DO
YOU HAVE TO KEEP MOVING
FORWARD."
Dr. Martin Luther
King Jr.

Healthy Tip Number Four

Exercise

Go merrily in the right way.
Be like a boat.
Balanced, strong, durable, always floating down stream,
Not against the current, not upstream.
You know what that means.
In all your chores, studies, work and play,
Understand Mother Nature,
Science and life's inspirational ways.
Sense your direction, listen to your inner voice.
Life will always give you options,
Life will always give you a choice.
Listen to find the answers...
Float down stream, slowly you go.
Always keep moving!
Stay afloat!
Enjoy your life,
Merrily, merrily, explore as you go.

Healthy Tip Number Five

Sleep

Get your sleep.

So important to do.

Get your sleep!

Sleep helps recover your body, making it resilient.

Nourishes it too.

It allows you to gain strength in your body.

Peace in your mind.

Elasticity in your skin.

Your spirit will come shining through.

Sleep reveals to us our dreams.

Sleep leads to creativity too.

Another world to explore, to discover while we are asleep.

To be on top of your game,

To be completely healthy, not feeling weak.

Get enough sleep,

And your mind, body and spirit will be healthy, wealthy and wise!

Get your sleep in order to be at your best when you rise.

Healthy Tip Number Six

Meditate

Quiet your mind.
Mediate daily, whether young or old.
To be still is to know.
Ideas come to you, like rain brings a
rainbow.
Kindness, harmony, health, laughter,
love and peace envelopes you in a
golden light.
Total ecstasy.
Rapturous delight.
This golden light will be with you forever.
Like a force field protecting and guiding you.
People will notice your great happiness.
They will want what you have.
You'll tell them to mediate.
To quite their mind,
Whether it be for a second, a minute or hours,
Mediate daily, learn to be still.
It will bring you magical powers.

"YOU DO NOT NEED TO LEAVE YOUR ROOM.
REMAIN SITTING AT YOUR TABLE AND LISTEN.
DO NOT EVEN LISTEN, SIMPLY WAIT, BE QUIET STILL AND SOLITARY.
THE WORLD WILL FREELY OFFER ITSELF TO YOU TO BE UNMASKED.
IT HAS NO OTHER CHOICE, IT WILL ROLL IN ECSTACY AT YOUR FEET."

Franz Kafka

"TO A MIND THAT IS STILL,
THE WHOLE UNIVERSE SURRENDERS."

Lao Tzu

Healthy Tip Number Seven

Don't Stress.

Relax into the World. Life is glorious and grand just the way she is.

Fame and gain, pain and sorrow.

Laughter, love and loss,

It is all part of living.

Don't stress.

Relax into the world.

Just do your best, with no expectations.

Do your best and be satisfied with what life brings you.

Don't stress.

Stress will bring you down both mentally and physically.

Stress will turn a smile into a frown.

Don't give in to stress.

Don't give in I say.

Release your struggles and let go.

Letting go is part of your

life, designed just for you,

Part of your way.

Don't stress,

Find what you love to do.

With no expectations,

Relax into the world,

Trust in the direction of

your beliefs,

The direction of your life.

Don't stress, simply....

Smile and turn that

frown back upside down!

designed by 🖤 freepik

Healthy Tip Number Eight
Be Adventurous

Look to what you dream of and go.

Go to where your mind, heart and spirit soar.

Go to your dreams, go there,

Go there now.

Dare to live your life fully.

Completely.

Sweetly.

Dare also to go to where you don't want to go as well.

It's alright to be frightened, to move slow,

To take a risk is so wise

Going towards what you fear with gusto and enthusiasm allows you to learn,

Allows you to grow.

One you get there; you'll be happy you went

At first reluctant, soon you'll find your time and endeavors well spent.

So, Dare, Dream, Discover.

Be adventurous, be daring and bold.

Even if it's just a little at first,

Face your challenges, face your fear.

Go for it.

Go for it with great perseverance,

Go with great cheer!

"LIFE IS EITHER A DARING ADVENTURE
OR NOTHING."

Helen Keller

If you can dream it you can do it

Healthy Tip Number Nine

Read

Read every day.
It helps you get smarter, in every way.
Read every day I say.
Settle in with a good book,
Be it on your phone, a computer or holding a book in your hands,
Keep reading.
Reading is fundamental.
You'll be glad you read.
It is simply important to do!
Whether for a moment or two,
Or maybe for hours and hours,
Read every day, I say.
You will learn and grow,
And oh, by the way,
Reading is cool and way fun too!

Healthy Tip Number Ten

Be a lifelong learner.

Be a lifelong learner.

Be it music, science, or arts.

Be it mathematics, engineering, technology, or sports

Be a lifelong learner.

Be like a sponge.

Soak it in.

Learn and have fun.

Remember it's what you learn after you know it all that counts.

So be a lifelong learner.

Know, ponder, explore and see.

Being a lifelong

learner is wonderful,

Continually learning is where you always want to be.

Healthy Tip Number Eleven

Eat well.

Eat well every day.

Be it fruits, veggies, pasta, proteins, fruits, nuts and grains,

Eat well every day.

It will keep your body and mind from decaying,

Within a healthy range,

Eating well will save you from an unhealthy change.

Eating healthy foods is smart, not lame.

Keep feeding your nourishing food,

Help maintain your incredible body we call machines,

Feed your body well,

You will feel lean and keen.

A well oiled machine!

Nourish yourself.

Eat well in every way.

Feed your body, your muscles, and your skin.

Feed your bones, organs and brain.

Eating well will help you to maintain.

It will put you at your best,

It will put you on top your game!

Healthy Tip Number Twelve
Stop feeling sorry for yourself

Everyone, everywhere is battling something.
Everyone everywhere.
No matter how famous, no matter how rich,
Whether you are struggling, or riding high with success.
Whether in a crowd or by yourself.
Everyone, everywhere is battling something,
In this you are not alone.
Many look like they have it all.
They'll smile and brag and preen.
Like they have it made. But...
Don't be so sure.
Don't be jealous
Everyone's' wants and desires are the same;
We all want to be heard,
To be seen.
Maybe your shy, sad and afraid to speak.
Maybe loud and boisterous, anxious to speak.
It is attention, acceptance and love we all seek.
Sometimes we hurt,
Sometimes we feel small.
Do not worry.
Do not fret.
Rejoice in the way things are!
Be content with what you have!
Do not feel sorry for yourself!
Be proud of you!
Be proud of everyone, because underneath it all.....
We are all the same!

DONT FEEL SORRY FOR YOURSELF
IF YOU HAVE CHOSEN THE WRONG PATH, CHOOSE ANOTHER.

Healthy Tip Number Thirteen
Charity.

Give Back.
Give time.
Give yourself.
Be kind.
It is by helping others,
Those less fortunate.
Those who have been left behind.
Lend them a helping hand.
Give them your kindness,
Give them your time.
No one knows anyone else's circumstances,
How they got lost.
How they got behind.
That doesn't matter.
Help them.
Reach out to them.
Be kind.
It will come back to you tenfold.
Your life will be rewarded.
You will see.
As long as you give from
your heart,
As long as you care.
Yours will be a virtuous
life,
A life that is peaceful,
happy and free.

Healthy Tip Number Fourteen
Friendship

Make friendship a fine art.
Do it today.
If you haven't yet,
Start! Start this moment, start right a way.
Do not take your friends, your mates, your amigos and amigas for granted.
They have been brought into your life, on purpose,
So you are never stranded.
They have been brought into your life on purpose,
Not randomly, but by design.
To laugh with you, to cry with you.
To ride life's emotional roller coaster with each other .
Learning together, learning apart,
Sometimes we become friends right from the start.
Be it through internet or spontaneous banter,
Maybe going on adventures with your friends,
Or hanging out in your backyard by the fence.
It just doesn't get any better when you are with your friends.
Nor does it matter the number of friends you have.
Matters not at all, to you or to them.
It's about the loyalty, trust and depth of your friendship,
Helping your friends in any way,
Whether boosting you up, or you them,
Catching you when you fall,
Catching them as well.
Together, living with honesty, communication, compassion, integrity and love,
True friendship will help you soar to any occasion,

To enjoy your life...
To always rise above.

designed by freepik.com

Healthy Tip Number Fifteen
Confidence

You are enough.
Remember that always.
You are enough.
You need nothing more than to be yourself.
There is no need to be arrogant, or condescending in any way.
You are no better nor worse than anyone else, in any form, in any way.
Whether it be yesterday, tomorrow or today.
Just being yourself will allow you to believe,
That you have all talent and confidence you need
Let go of comparisons,
Just be yourself.
Believe, have confidence in who you are.
Go confidently in your direction and your dreams,
Having confidence will take you far.
Know that you can and will succeed.
With hard work, you will...
Achieve all you wish, all you can vision,
All you can perceive.
Have unwavering strength in
your capabilities,
In this -
You Must Believe.

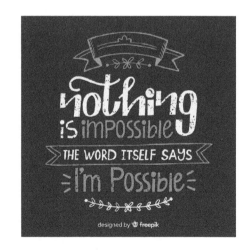

Healthy Tip Number Sixteen

Balance

Life is a balance.

A dance.

A play.

Sometimes you are up, sometimes you are down.

Sometimes you go the right way,

Other times, it simply isn't your day.

Don't take it personally.

Don't quit or give up.

Don't fret, cry or pout.

Everything always works itself out.

Life is balance.

Life is that way.

The bad will pass,

The good will not last.

History teaches us, leaves clues, her lessons are profound.

Know and understand these lessons of balance,

Give and take.

Knowing this will keep you on solid ground.

Make no mistake,

At work or at play,

Practice balance in all

you do, think and say.

Practicing balance

daily, both spiritu-

ally, physically and

mentally,....

Leads to a better way.

Healthy Tip Number Seventeen
Yoga

Yoga is fun!
Whether you have done it for years, or just begun.
You can sit, or stand, stretch and hop,
Yoga helps you to tune in to yourself,
To tune into your life.
To ease your pain,
To ease your strife.
Yoga helps you manage your surroundings,
Yoga helps manage your life.
You will learn to focus
To be aware
To be alive.
To know what is profound.
To know the differences between right and wrong.
Yoga makes you totally strong!
Yoga is fun, providing you with movement, harmony, balance and breath
Yoga will help you in every way, every day.
Yoga is a recipe for success!

Healthy Tip Number Eighteen
Workout

Add cardio to your life

Lift weights too.

It will make you smile, help your body feel alive!

You can do anything, run a marathon, do a triathlon, or complete an amazing high dive!

Walking, swimming, biking or jumping rope, it makes no difference, None at all.

Just remember to get your cardio and muscle- resisting exercises in, Your body and mind can tell,

That it's feeling fit, feeling strong, feeling well!

So go bike, run, swim and lift,

Get it all in, and...

Let the fun begin!

Healthy Tip Number Nineteen
Gratitude

Gratitude is everything in life.

With gratitude, you will have less strife.

It will bring a delightful spirit to your soul.

A feeling of total wellness, of being whole.

Focus on how blessed and lucky you truly are.

Focus on your fortunes, not your disappointments or fears.

Even when it all seems bad, when you have little,

Remember that this too shall pass.

For every bad there is good,

For every night, soon there is light.

Focus on your blessings and rejoice,

Know that by counting your blessings with gratitude,

All will be perfect,

All will be right!

Healthy Tip Number Twenty
Learn to Fail

Learn to fail.
Trust the process,
Trust the wait.
Fall down seven times,
Get up eight!
Learn to fail, over and over and over again.
Keep falling,
Keep failing.
But....
Keep getting back up again.
Without failure, you cannot learn
Only failure can lead to a positive and direct turn.
A turn to what you now know,
A path,
Positive directions to follow.
Failure will teach
you to keep trying,
To never give up.
Failure is the wise
sages' drinking cup.

Healthy Tip Number Twenty-One
Be Peaceful

Peace is tranquility, calmness and poise.
Peace is living in the moment, in stillness.
It is the quieting of the mind,
The removal of outside chatter and noise.
It is a recipe for health and wellness.
Seek to be peaceful, today, tomorrow,
Always.

Healthy Tip Number Twenty-Two
Happiness

To be happy is a conscious choice.

Being happy is smart, never a mistake.

Even when it's hard,

Even when your body shakes.

Even when your are crying, sad and scared.

When life doesn't seem fair.

Choosing happiness will always be your ticket out of despair.

When you are down and can't possibly seem to be able to get back up,

When you can't see yourself ever being stable and sound.

This is the toughest time, the time when you are really down.

That's when you stop, you slow down, you get back up.

You start to help others, this is key.

Helping others shows us the way to be happy, now and every day.

Knowing to give to others will lead you to happiness.

Whether by donating your time or monies to charities or helping people you know.

Maybe volunteering in person, it doesn't matter how you help,

Matters not at all.

Strive to be happy,

Let happiness be your daily goal.

"HAPPINESS NOT IN ANOTHER PLACE
BUT THIS PLACE
NOT FOR ANOTHER HOUR
BUT THIS HOUR"

Walt Whitman

Healthy Tip Number Twenty-Three

Courage

To be courageous is to be yourself.
Courage to appreciate who you are.
Courage to go for it all.
No matter how tall or short,
No matter how big or small you are,
It makes no matter at all.
Courage knows no size.
Have the courage to go out on a limb.
Lean into life for all it has to give.
At first you might fall, stumble or crawl.
But maybe, just maybe you'll soar and fly, you'll be on a roll!
So be courageous,
Be courageous, give it a whirl.
Be courageous,
Go on give it a try!

Healthy Tip Number Twenty-Four

Love

Love.
Love yourself.
Love others.
Love the bad.
Love the good.
Love your friends.
Love your family.
Love your enemies.
Love the present.
Love the past.
Love where you want to go.
Love where you've been.
Love where you are.
Love it all, whether near or far.
Love is your mainsail.
Love is your rod and staff.
Love gets rid of strife.
Love lets you laugh!
Love is the best
Love will bring you a smile,
Love leads to a wonderful life!

designed by 🌸 freepik

Healthy Tip Number Twenty-Five

Music

Learn to love and relish music.
Music is a wonderful teacher,
A wonderful gift!
Whether singing a song with a strong voice, or
Playing an instrument of your choice.
Learn to embrace music.
Embrace it and love it.
Music brings joy all day long.
Whether through an instrument or through song.
Perfecting an instrument is so gratifying.
It's not easy.
But nothing worthwhile in life is.
We all know that practice makes perfect,
Practice is wise.
Practice teaches us the value of repeating something over and over,
Again and again.
At first it will seem boring, but trust the process,
Stay the course.
You will see your improvement daily.
Learning and practicing music will help you grow..
Play and practice what instrument you want.
Play and practice every day.
Whether the guitar, violin, oboe, drums, or your voice in song.
No matter what you choose, the more you learn, the more skills you
will have to use.
Music teaches us the rhythms and rhymes of life,
It reduces our stress, our strife.
The more music you learn, the more you'll want to play.

Music is wonderful,
Begin Now,
Begin Today,
Music is wonderful!
Music is the way!

Healthy Tip Number Twenty-Six
Tranquility

Be calm.

Be well.

Be peaceful.

Be still.

Be tranquil.

Tranquility is yours to have.

Tranquility is yours to create.

Tranquility lies within you.

Tranquility is your true state.

A searching within.

A searching of the soul, spirit and mind.

Tranquility is an important practice that is yours to find.

Be tranquil and shine!

Healthy Tip Number Twenty-Seven

Listen

Two ears and one mouth,
That's what we have.
That's who we are.
It makes sense to listen twice as much.
Listen while others speak.
Listen to their pause between each word., each inflection they speak.
Listen and you will be surprised,
You'll realize how much you hear,
And you will surmise
Listening is knowledge.
Listening is the key.
Listening is wise.

Healthy Tip Number Twenty-Eight

Ecology

Mother Earth is our home,
Our friend
Our Planet.
Our source.
To protect her in every way, is our duty.
We must protect Mother Earth every moment, every day.
It is truly our mission,
All of us.
Together.
Our responsibility is to each other.
To help save our home.
We need clean air and clean water to survive.
We need a healthy planet for all of us to thrive!
We must accept that climate change is real.
Collectively we can save our
future,
Restore our home.
It is our most important mission,
Our greatest task.
We must do this together,
All around our Earth
Together, not alone.
We must all protect Mother
Earth, our home.

Healthy Tip Number Twenty-Nine
Stop Judgment

Stop judgment of all kind,
Whether judging yourself or others.
Stop judging,
Don't do it
Just let it go
Don't judge.
It leads no where.
Nowhere at all.
We are all spiritual beings having a
human experience.
We are all creatures on our magnifi-
cent planet, Mother Earth.
Together, we are one.
Splendid spirits enjoying life, learning, exploring, having fun.
We are all the same you and me.
Staying together non judgmentally can help us.
This we understand,
This we can all see.
Staying together will help provide safety and security for us all.
Not judging whether someone is important or not,
Whether someone is big or small.
If we treat everything and everyone with respect.
If we treat everything and everyone the same,
Then together , today and tomorrow we will not judge,
We will refrain.
For together in life,
We are all the same.

Namaste
designed by 🕊 freepik.com

Healthy Tip Number Thirty

Work

Work hard.

Work hard every day.

Luck is where preparation meets opportunity.

With hard work, luck shows up everyday.

It is through time served.

It is your dedication, blood, sweat and toil.

This doesn't mean living a life that is abandoned of fun or spice, or being dull.

Do your best, try, that is all you need do.

Work and play go hand in hand, this we know.

So set your daily goal to always, always improve..

This formula of hard work is tried and true, it has been this way forever and ever.

Throughout the years.

Hard work leads to success for all.

This is life's clue..

Chapter Eleven

Mantras

Mantras are words or instruments of the mind. We use them in meditation. They are internally repeated. Mantras are instruments or tools to help keep our mind focused.

There purpose is to quiet the many thoughts one experiences during meditation.

Your brain will never be totally silent or still in meditation or in life.

A mantra will help you, allowing you to become more tranquil within.

When our minds constantly chatter, we sometimes refer to this as our monkey mind.

Like monkeys going from tree to tree, eating a single bite of a piece of fruit, never being satisfied, they keep continuing on to the next tree, the next fruit; hoping to find a better tasting delight in the next tree, the next bite.

But a mantra will help guide you back to your breath, to being still and tranquil.

A mantra can be truly profound.

So instead of going from tree to tree, from fruit to fruit, enjoy your meditation quietly.

To mediate, is to find stillness and contentment.

This quietness lets you explore what lies within.

Knowing no bounds, you will begin to discover wisdom beyond measure.

So use your mantra to help quiet the many chattering thoughts away.

Meditating daily leads to a peaceful life in many, many beneficial ways.

Here is a List of Mantras

I am grateful.

I am that I am.

I am honoring the divine within me.

I am peace.

I am love.

I am compassion.

I am happy.

I am healthy.

I am calm.

I am you.

I am me.

I am bliss.

I am tranquility.

I am space.

I am life.

I am strong.

I am non judgmental.

I am here.

I am space.

I am present.

I am aware.

I dwell in possibilities.

I am industrious.

I am motivated.

I am lucky.

I am alive.

I am the Universe.

I am happy

I am joy

I am healthy

I am strong as a mountain

I am loving

I am kind

We are all one

I believe

I let go

I am here

It is now

I am truth

I Explore

I am humble

All is well

All is perfect

I have a purpose

I am prosperous

I am relaxed

I am at ease

Sanskrit Mantras

Om Shanti—I am peaceful

Karuna Ham—I am compassion

Sat, Chit, Ananda—truth, consciousness, bliss

So Ham—I am, I am honoring the divine within me

Ananda Ham—I am bliss

Rasa Ham—The juiciness of life

Sa,(Birth) Ta,(Life) Na,(Death), Ma, (Rebirth)

Chapter Twelve

Yoga Games

Here is a list of useful and fun yoga games for teachers, students, family and friends.

Some take only a few minutes. Others are longer,

It's up to the players to say when they are done, to say it's time for this game to end.

Every yoga student needs to have some fun.

Some games you can play either inside or under the stars or sun.

Yoga games provides lessons for us all.

For both students and teachers, families too, It's just a cool thing to do.

Participating with each other,

Exploring the poses together, Like a team in unison, that's the path way.

The meaning of yoga is together, a union, one with each other.

Older or young, yoga games teach wonderful lessons,

Yoga shows us that we are all the same.

Yoga games will stimulate your body,

Yoga games will stimulate your brain.

Yoga games brings everyone together,

That is how the world should be,

Together, as one.

Game One

Red Light Game

Red light Green light
Let the fun begin!
First your teacher tells you to walk or run,
Your teacher than shouts red light.
You stop,
You must do the yoga pose your teacher chooses.
Whether Tree or Warrior One,
It matters not
Just pretend you are the pose your teacher suggests you be.
Have fun in this pose, practice this pose, become the pose,
And you will see
How the game Red light, Green light is supposed to be played.
Start this fun game, don't delay.,
You will want to play all day!
You'll have fun, you'll see.
Again the teacher shouts green light once more, then red and the pose changes to another.
So run, run, run. smile, smile, smile!
There'll be plenty of poses for you to do,
More fun, more glee!

Game Two
The Tickle Game

Get the kids lying down, forming a circle
A head on someone else's tummy, this is going to be funny!
With everyone's head on their friends belly
Someone now begins to tickle the first kid on the floor
Soon with laughter, like dominoes falling, the laughter spreads as they
feel their belly's rising up and down, vibrating together
They laugh, they roar.
Laughing so hard and smiling with delight,
They move and squirm like jelly,
Oh what fun!
Oh what a sight!

The Breathing Game

Place a toy animal on your stomachs and chest.
As you breath, watch and feel the rise and fall of your toy.
Inhaling, filling your lungs up, full and complete
Exhaling the old air out, notice how good you feel.
Wow slow breathing is healthy and fun
Breathing in and out is sweet!
What a treat!
This game shows us the value of our breath,
One breath at a time
By doing this, you are really teaching yourself meditation,
How to quiet your mind, how to be peaceful and content and,
How to have fun!

Chapter Thirteen

This is Your Story; This is My Story

You now know my story; my continuous health issues and my continuous journey to get a little bit better every day.

I wrote this book for you, and hopefully this will inspire you to believe in yourself, to work hard, to be kind, kind to yourself and kind to all others.

To persevere.

To be able to overcome.

To learn from all of life's' challenges, all of life's' tests.

We all have issues. We all have choices too.

Choices to either quit, give up, or cry in self pity.

Or...

To choose to work hard and simply, Try! To improve our lives, we simply must utilize every ounce of strength and courage we can muster.

By continually moving forward, nor matter how slow, or tedious, or hard our challenges are, we must keep moving forward.

We must keep asking ourselves; "What can I do to get better?"

This such an important question to continually ask yourself, "What can I do... to improve, to get better, to feel better, to be happier, to overcome my challenges?" For me, at 22 years old, as I lay in my hospital bed after my first back operation, (by then my second of 16 major operations) in utter misery and pain, the question I continually asked myself was...

"What can I do to feel better, to improve, to make my back stronger?"

I didn't want to go through four more back operations as my doctors said I would, so I kept asking myself the magical question, "What can I do to get better?". (This a question I now ask myself after every operation and every procedure). As I began to explore my options, the answer came to me when I remembered being introduced to yoga by Torbin Ulrich, (Thank you Mr. Ulrich!) just mere months before my back injury. Yoga came into my life and saved me. I am forever indebted to Mr. Ulrich, a truly amazing renaissance man!

I am forever grateful to the nurses, doctors and physical therapists who were so kind, inspirational and nurturing!

I am grateful to all my amazing teachers, especially my first teacher, Ethel Mercer. Thank you Ethel! My body has been an ongoing challenge. As a result of my deteriorating spine, many doctors can't really understand how I am able to do all that I do. Many doctors cannot understand how I can even move without pain and agony.

The answer is simple:

BE POSITIVE.

BE PROACTIVE.

FIND A WAY.

IMPROVE EVERY DAY

Because of my facial deformities as I previously mentioned, I have also had to adjust to people looking at me funny, to get use to my different looking countenance. Around nine or ten, my face and smile became crooked. Doctors speculate that this was a result of Bell's Palsy or Polio, or a horse riding accident I had when I was young. Truly no one knows for sure.

Regardless of the diagnosis, this facial difference has greatly, (and with much pain and anguish), affected me over my entire life.

My crooked face and smile, and my odd right eye, is, as they say, not a recipe for perfect looks! My right eye does not completely close, hence my eye color is constantly red!

It doesn't take a brilliant mind to see why kids continually ask me

"What's up with you, Why do you look like that?" "What happened to you?"

Trust me, even after a million times of hearing this, it's still uncomfortable.

This has led to many insecurities, fear, failure and anxiety.

But Like All Of Us,

We all face our own unique set of challenges, whether it be mental, physical or both. We must seek the ways to overcome our issues.

Wherever we are, what ever we have or don't have, we cannot allow ourselves to wallow in self pity.

It is simply the cards we are dealt in life.

This is the reason I have written this book, to help others struggling with their confidence, physical challenges and low self esteem, to get better, to overcome, to believe in themselves.

It is through many lessons learned that I realized that I must continually, and will always...

Work on Solutions to My Problems.

To Make Lemonade From Lemons!

I am here to share with you, that you need only to embrace your differences, to relish in them and see them as positives, not as negatives, to view them as a guide to improving and becoming better.

To you I say....

Embrace your differences.

Conquer your fears and obstacles.

Via La Difference!

A Traves De La Diferencia!

Appreciate your Differences!

Appreciate WHO YOU ARE!

CHOOSE TO LIVE THE VERY BEST LIFE YOU CAN LIVE

"BE WHO YOU ARE AND SAY WHAT YOU FEEL BECAUSE THOSE WHO MIND DON'T MATTER
AND THOSE WHO MATTER DON'T MIND."

Dr. Seuss

May you be free from suffering

May you be happy

May you love and be loved

May you find peace

May you be at ease

Namaste'

Respectfully,

Michael Zerner

Acknowledgments

"I have had the good fortune to be raised by two wonderful and extraordinary parents. They taught me many insightful and invaluable life lessons. These lessons have enabled me to live my life in an extraordinary way. To fight the good fight and live everyday to the best of my abilities. These lessons have instilled in me the curiosity of life, the rights and wrongs of life, the ups and downs of life and the values of living a life with integrity, honesty, kindness, compassion, community service, adventure, education, love of sports, and so much more. My Mom and Dad gave me love and kindness when I needed it. They gave me tough love, discipline and understanding when I needed it.

They gave so much, to so many, selflessly.

Thank you Mom and Dad!

I am forever grateful!

Thank you to all the wonderful people who helped with this book, I couldn't have done this without you!

To Amy Buckey and Colleen Dunn Bates for helping me find a publisher.

To Paul Cohen of Epigraph Publishing and Colin Rolfe of Monkfish Book Publishing for all their help and guidance.

Thank you to Amy Buckey, Julie Shapiro, Carol Schwab, Eric Puszczewicz, Judy Szor, Renee Watkins, Helena Eddings, Meggan Kucsma, Hannah Shariff, Ronnie Thompson , Therese King and

Ananta Ajmera for looking over my manuscript and telling me to keep going, keep writing, and that it doesn't stink!

Thank you to Shirley Joseph, The Grand Dame of yoga in Toledo, Ohio, for giving me the inspiration to find the format for my book, for her knowledge, kindness, compassion and friendship. You are truly what yoga represents Shirley, thank you!

LAST, BUT NOT LEAST...

I cannot Thank Eric Puszczewicz enough! He has helped make this book far better than the original.

His guidance, creativity, thoughtfulness and incredible computer and marketing skills are heaven sent.

Michael Zerner is a yoga teacher. He lives in Toledo, Ohio with his best friend, a beautiful White Shepherd/Golden Labrador rescue dog named Genna.

Thank you Genna for truly rescuing me!

CPSIA information can be obtained
at www.ICGtesting.com
Printed in the USA
JSHW040924030721
16531JS00005B/14